STANDUP

SALESPERSO

N:

Crafting a Wining Strategy for Lasting Business Relationships

ISRAEL .O

COPYRIGHT PAGE

TABLE OF CONTENTS

INTRODUCTION

The world of sales is constantly evolving, and with the rise of technology and changing consumer behaviors, it's more important than ever for sales professionals to have a solid strategy in place. In "Standup Salesperson: Crafting a Winning Strategy for Lasting Business Relationship," we explore the various techniques and tactics that successful salespeople use to connect with customers, build relationships, and close deals. From crafting a compelling pitch to leveraging technology and analyzing sales metrics, this comprehensive guide offers practical advice and actionable insights for anyone looking to improve their sales game. Whether you're a seasoned sales professional or just starting out in the field, "The Standup Act of a Good Salesperson" is an invaluable resource that will help you achieve your goals and succeed in today's competitive marketplace.

Definition of the Standup Act of a Good Salesperson

The standup act of a good salesperson is a performance or presentation given by a salesperson that is engaging, persuasive and informative. This act is designed to capture the attention of potential customers and convince them to purchase a product or service. A good salesperson will use humor, storytelling, and other techniques to build rapport with the audience and create a memorable experience that will leave a lasting impression. The act should be original and tailored to the specific customer targets.

Importance of Having a Sales Strategy

Sales strategy is an essential component of any marketing plan. It is a comprehensive plan that outlines the steps to be taken to achieve sales goals. A sales strategy is essential because it helps businesses to identify their target audience, develop a sales plan, and implement it effectively. In this article, we will discuss the importance of having a sales strategy in marketing.

1. Helps to Identify the Target Audience:
One of the primary benefits of having a sales strategy is that it helps businesses to identify their target audience. A sales strategy enables businesses to understand the needs, preferences, and behaviors of their potential customers. By knowing their target audience, businesses can develop products and services that meet their customers' needs. This, in turn, leads to increased sales and revenue.

2. Provides a Clear Sales Plan:

Having a sales strategy provides a clear plan of action for businesses to follow. It outlines the steps that need to be taken to achieve sales goals. A sales plan includes identifying the target audience, developing a marketing message, setting sales targets, and developing a sales process. With a clear sales plan, businesses can focus their efforts on achieving their sales goals.

3. Helps to Allocate Resources Efficiently:

A sales strategy helps businesses to allocate their resources efficiently. By identifying their target audience and developing a sales plan, businesses can allocate their resources to the areas that will generate the most revenue. This ensures that businesses do not waste resources on activities that do not contribute to their sales goals.

4. Enables Effective Sales Management:

Having a sales strategy enables effective sales management. Sales managers can use the sales strategy to monitor sales performance and make adjustments as necessary. By tracking sales performance, sales managers can identify areas that need improvement and take corrective action.

STANDUP
SALESPERSON:
Crafting a Winning Strategy for Lasting Business Relationships

This ensures that businesses are always on track to achieve their sales goals.

5. Improves Customer Satisfaction:
A sales strategy helps businesses to develop products and services that meet their customers' needs. By understanding their target audience, businesses can develop products and services that are tailored to their customers' preferences. This leads to increased customer satisfaction and loyalty. Satisfied customers are more likely to recommend the business to others, which can lead to increased sales and revenue.

In conclusion, having a sales strategy is essential for businesses that want to achieve their sales goals. A sales strategy helps businesses to identify their target audience, develop a sales plan, allocate resources efficiently, enable effective sales management, and improve customer satisfaction. By implementing a sales strategy, businesses can increase their sales and revenue, and ultimately achieve long-term success.

BUILDING A STRONG FOUNDATION

Building a strong foundation in business is crucial for any organization or individual looking to achieve success in the competitive world of business. This foundation involves several key elements, including a strong understanding of marketing, sales, and customer service. In this context, a good salesperson is someone who has mastered the art of selling and understands how to build and maintain strong relationships with customers.

One real marketing situation that highlights the importance of building a strong foundation in business is the case of Coca-Cola. Coca-Cola is a global brand that has been around for over a century. The company has built a strong foundation in business by focusing on its core values, which include quality, integrity, and innovation. Coca-Cola's marketing strategy is centered on its famous logo and brand image, which is recognized worldwide. The company has built a strong relationship with its customers by consistently delivering high-quality products and services.

Another real marketing situation that illustrates the importance of building a strong foundation in business is the case of Apple. Apple is a technology company that has revolutionized the way we use technology in our daily lives. The company has built a strong foundation in business by focusing on innovation, design, and user experience. Apple's marketing strategy is centered on its iconic products, such as the iPhone, iPad, and MacBook. The company has built a strong relationship with its customers by consistently delivering innovative products that meet their needs and exceed their expectations.

A good salesperson plays a critical role in building a strong foundation in business. A good salesperson understands the needs of their customers and knows how to build and maintain strong relationships with them. They are knowledgeable about their products and services and can effectively communicate their value to customers. A good salesperson is also able to anticipate the needs of their customers and provide them with solutions that meet those needs.

Building a strong foundation in business is essential for achieving success in the competitive world of business. Real marketing situations such as those of Coca-Cola and Apple highlight the importance of core values, innovation, and customer relationships in building a strong foundation. A good salesperson plays a critical role in this process by understanding the needs of their customers and building lasting relationships with them. By focusing on these key elements, organizations and individuals can build a strong foundation in business that will enable them to achieve long term success

Understanding Your Product or Service

Understanding your product or service is essential to the success of any business. It is crucial to have a thorough understanding of what you are offering to your customers, as it can impact your sales, customer satisfaction, and overall reputation. In this chapter, we will explore the importance of understanding your product or service and how it can help you succeed in today's competitive marketplace.

Firstly, it is essential to understand the features and benefits of your product or service. This involves knowing its unique selling points, how it compares to similar products or services in the market, and what sets it apart from the competition. Understanding these features and benefits allows you to effectively communicate them to potential customers, which can help you to convert leads into sales.

Secondly, it is crucial to understand your target audience. This involves identifying the specific needs and wants of your customers and how your product or service can meet those needs. By understanding your target audience, you can tailor your marketing efforts to reach them effectively and provide them with a personalized experience.

Thirdly, it is essential to understand the value proposition of your product or service. This involves understanding the perceived value of your product or service in the eyes of your customers. By understanding the value proposition, you can price your product or service appropriately and ensure that it is competitive in the market.

In addition to these factors, it is also important to understand the limitations of your product or service. This involves knowing its weaknesses and potential areas for improvement. By understanding these limitations, you can work to address them and improve your product or service over time.

Overall, understanding your product or service is essential to the success of your business. By knowing its features and benefits, target audience, value proposition, and limitations, you can effectively market and sell your product or service, improve customer satisfaction, and ultimately achieve success in today's competitive marketplace.

Identifying Your Target Market

To develop an effective marketing strategy for your business, it is essential to identify your target market audience. This refers to a Particular group of individuals who are most likely to show interest in your product or service.

By understanding who your target audience is, you can tailor your marketing efforts to reach them effectively and provide them with a personalized experience. In this chapter, we will explore the importance of identifying your target audience and how to do so effectively.

Firstly, it is essential to conduct market research to identify your target audience. This involves gathering data on your potential customers, such as their age, gender, income, location, interests, and behaviors. You can gather this data through surveys, focus groups, online analytics tools, and other market research methods. By analyzing this data, you can gain insights into the characteristics and behaviors of your target audience, which can help you to develop a more effective marketing strategy.

Secondly, it is important to create buyer personas to represent your target audience. A buyer persona is an imaginary individual that embodies the characteristics of your perfect customer. . It includes information such as their demographics, interests, motivations, challenges, and goals. By creating buyer personas, you can better understand the needs and wants of your target audience and tailor your marketing efforts to meet those needs.

Thirdly, it is crucial to consider the buying journey of your target audience. This involves understanding the different stages that your potential customers go through when making a purchasing decision. By understanding these stages, you can create marketing content that is tailored to each stage of the buying journey, from awareness to consideration to decision-making.

In addition to these factors, it is also important to consider the competition in your market. By analyzing your competitors and their target audiences, you can identify gaps in the market and potential opportunities to reach new customers.

Overall, identifying your target audience is essential to the success of your marketing strategy. By conducting market research, creating buyer personas, considering the buying journey, and analyzing the competition, you can develop a more effective and personalized approach to marketing your product or service.

Researching the Competition

Researching the competition is an essential step in developing a successful marketing strategy for your business. By analyzing your competitors, you can gain insights into their strengths and weaknesses, identify potential opportunities and threats, and develop a more effective and competitive approach to marketing your product or service. In this chapter, we will explore the importance of researching the competition and how to do so effectively, using existing organizations as examples.

Firstly, it is essential to identify your competitors. This involves researching other organizations that offer similar products or services to yours. You can use online directories, industry reports, and search engines to identify your competitors. Once you have identified your competitors, you can analyze their marketing strategies, strengths, and weaknesses.

For example, let's say you are launching a new coffee shop in a busy city center. Your competitors may include other coffee shops in the area, as well as chain coffee shops like Starbucks and Costa. By analyzing their marketing strategies, you can gain insights into what works and what doesn't in your market. You can also identify potential opportunities and threats, such as a new competitor entering the market or changing consumer preferences.

Secondly, it is important to analyze your competitors' strengths and weaknesses. This involves researching their products or services, pricing strategies, marketing efforts, and customer feedback. By analyzing their strengths and weaknesses, you can identify potential areas for improvement in your own business.

For example, by researching Starbucks and Costa, you may find that they have a strong brand reputation and a loyal customer base. However, they may also have higher prices than your coffee shop and may not offer the same level of personalized service. By identifying these strengths and weaknesses, you can develop a unique value proposition for your coffee shop and tailor your marketing efforts to reach a different audience.

Thirdly, it is crucial to monitor your competitors' marketing efforts over time. This involves keeping up-to-date with their social media accounts, website updates, and advertising campaigns. By monitoring their marketing efforts, you can identify changes in their strategy and respond accordingly.

For example, if one of your competitors launches a new advertising campaign, you may need to adjust your own marketing efforts to remain competitive.

You may also identify potential areas for improvement in your own marketing strategy by analyzing what works and what doesn't for your competitors.

In conclusion, researching the competition is essential to the success of your marketing strategy. By identifying your competitors, analyzing their strengths and weaknesses, and monitoring their marketing efforts over time, you can develop a more effective and competitive approach to marketing your product or service.

CRAFTING YOUR MESSAGE

Crafting a message as a sales standup marketer is a critical skill for winning strategic and lasting business customer relationships. The message that you deliver to potential customers can make a significant difference in whether they choose to do business with you or not. In this chapter, we will explore the importance of crafting a message that resonates with your target audience and how to do so effectively.

To begin with, it is crucial to comprehend your intended audience by recognizing their requirements, desires, and areas of concern. By understanding your target audience, you can tailor your message to meet their specific needs and provide them with a personalized experience.

Secondly, it is important to develop a unique value proposition. A value proposition is a statement that explains why your product or service is unique and why customers should choose you over your competitors. By developing a compelling value proposition, you can differentiate yourself from your competitors and provide a clear reason for potential customers to choose you.

Thirdly, it is crucial to focus on the benefits of your product or service rather than just its features. Customers are more interested in how your product or service can benefit them rather than just its technical specifications. By focusing on the benefits, you can appeal to the emotional needs of your target audience and provide them with a reason to choose you over your competitors.

In addition to these factors, it is also important to use storytelling to engage your audience. By telling a story that resonates with your target audience, you can create an emotional connection and build trust with them. You can use case studies, testimonials, and personal experiences to tell your story and demonstrate the value of your product or service.

Overall, crafting a message as a sales standup marketer is essential to winning strategic and lasting business customer relationships. By understanding your target audience, developing a unique value proposition, focusing on the benefits, and using storytelling, you can create a message that resonates with your potential customers and provides them with a compelling reason to choose you over your competitors.

Developing a Compelling Pitch

Developing a winning and compelling marketing pitch is a critical skill for sales standup marketers. A marketing pitch is a brief and persuasive message that explains the benefits of your product or service and why customers should choose you over your competitors. A compelling marketing pitch can help you capture the attention of potential customers, build trust with them, and ultimately win their business. In this chapter, we will explore the importance of developing a winning and compelling marketing pitch and how to do so effectively.

To begin with, it is crucial to comprehend your intended audience by recognizing their requirements, desires, and areas of concern.. By understanding your target audience, you can tailor your marketing pitch to meet their specific needs and provide them with a personalized experience.

Secondly, it is important to develop a unique selling proposition. A unique selling proposition is a statement that explains what sets your product or service apart from your competitors and why customers should choose you. By developing a compelling unique selling proposition, you can differentiate yourself from your competitors and provide a clear reason for potential customers to choose you.

Thirdly, it is crucial to focus on the benefits of your product or service rather than just its features. Customers are more interested in how your product or service can benefit them rather than just its technical specifications. By focusing on the benefits, you can appeal to the emotional needs of your target audience and provide them with a reason to choose you over your competitors.

In addition to these factors, it is also important to use a brand promise to engage your audience. Your brand promise is a statement that communicates what your brand stands for and what customers can expect from your product or service. By using a brand promise, you can create an emotional connection and build trust with your target audience.

Finally, it is crucial to practice your marketing pitch and refine it over time. You should be able to deliver your pitch confidently and effectively in any situation, whether it's in person, over the phone, or in a presentation. You should also be open to feedback and willing to make changes to your pitch based on what works and what doesn't.

Overall, developing a winning and compelling marketing pitch is essential to success as a sales stand up marketer. By understanding your target audience, developing a unique selling proposition, focusing on the benefits, using a brand promise, and practicing and refining your pitch over time, you can capture the attention of potential customers, build trust with them, and ultimately win their busin

Using Storytelling to Connect with Customers

The art of storytelling has been an integral aspect of human culture for centuries.. From the earliest cave paintings to the latest blockbuster movie, people have always been drawn to stories. But did you know that storytelling can also be a powerful tool for businesses? In fact, using storytelling to connect with customers is becoming increasingly popular.

In a world where consumers are bombarded with advertising and marketing messages, it can be difficult for businesses to stand out. But by telling a compelling story, businesses can capture their audience's attention and create a deeper connection with their customers.

Why does storytelling work?

Humans are hardwired to respond to stories. Our brains are naturally drawn to narratives, and we are more likely to remember information that is presented in a story format. Additionally, stories can evoke emotions and create a sense of empathy, which can help to build trust and loyalty.

How can businesses use storytelling?

There are many ways that businesses can incorporate storytelling into their marketing strategies. Here are a few examples:

1. Brand storytelling: This involves telling the story of your brand, including its history, values, and mission. By sharing your brand's story, you can create a sense of authenticity and build trust with your customers.

2. Customer stories: Highlighting the experiences of your customers can be a powerful way to connect with potential customers. Sharing testimonials, case studies, or success stories can help to build social proof and demonstrate the value of your product or service.

3. Employee stories: Telling the stories of your employees can help to humanize your brand and create a sense of community. Sharing stories about your team members can also help to showcase your company culture and values.

4. Product stories: Telling the story of how your product was created, or the problem it solves, can help to create a sense of excitement and intrigue.

By framing your product in a narrative context, you can make it more compelling and memorable.

Using storytelling to connect with customers is a powerful way for businesses to stand out in a crowded marketplace. By telling compelling stories, businesses can create a deeper connection with their customers and build trust and loyalty. Whether it's through brand storytelling, customer stories, employee stories, or product stories, there are many ways that businesses can incorporate storytelling into their marketing strategies.

MASTERING SALES TECHNIQUES

Sales are an essential part of any business, and mastering sales techniques can be the key to success. Whether you're selling a product or a service, it's important to have a solid understanding of the sales process and the techniques that can help you close deals.

Here are some tips for mastering sales techniques:

1. Listen to your customers

Being able to listen is considered one of the most crucial skills in sales. By listening to your customers, you can understand their needs and tailor your pitch to meet those needs. It is recommended to ask open-ended questions and genuinely pay attention to the responses provided. This will help you to build rapport and establish trust with your customers.

2. Build relationships

Sales are all about building relationships. Individuals tend to be inclined towards purchasing from someone they have faith in and find likable.

Take the time to get to know your customers and build a relationship with them.

3. Focus on benefits, not features

When selling a product or service, it's important to focus on the benefits, not just the features. Rather than simply knowing the features of your product or service, customers are interested in understanding how it can benefit them. Highlight the benefits of your product or service and show your customers how it can make their lives easier or better.

4. Use social proof

Social proof is a powerful tool in sales. People are more likely to buy something if they see that other people have bought it and are happy with it. Use testimonials, case studies, and reviews to show your customers that your product or service is worth buying.

5. Overcome objections

Encountering objections is a common occurrence in the sales process. Learn how to overcome objections by addressing them head-on. Listen to your customer's objections and respond with empathy. Demonstrate to them how your product or service can address their concerns or fulfill their requirements.

6. Close the deal

The ultimate objective of any sales pitch is to secure the deal. Learn how to close the deal by asking for the sale. Use trial closes to gauge your customer's interest and ask for the sale when the time is right.

Mastering sales techniques is essential for anyone in business. By listening to your customers, building relationships, focusing on benefits, using social proof, overcoming objections, and closing the deal, you can increase your sales and build a successful business. Whether you're a seasoned sale professional or just starting out, these tips can help you to master the art of sales.

Active Listening and Questioning: The Approach of a Standup Salesman

In the world of sales, communication is everything. The ability to actively listen to your customers and ask the right questions can be the key to closing deals and building long-term relationships. In this book, we will explore the active listening and questioning approach of a standup salesman.

Active Listening

Active listening is the process of fully concentrating on, understanding, and responding to what someone else is saying. In sales, active listening is essential for understanding your customer's needs and tailoring your pitch to meet those needs.

Here are some tips for active listening:

1. Pay attention: Give your customer your full attention. Pay attention to their words and avoid getting distracted.

2. Show interest: Show your customer that you are interested in what they have to say. Ask follow-up questions and show empathy.

3. Paraphrase: Repeat back what your customer has said in your own words. This shows that you understand and helps to clarify any misunderstandings.

4. Take notes: Taking notes can help you to remember important details and show your customer that you are serious about meeting their needs.

Questioning

Asking the right questions is essential for understanding your customer's needs and tailoring your pitch to meet those needs. Here are some tips for effective questioning:

1. Open-ended questions: Ask open-ended questions that encourage your customer to share more information. Avoid yes or no questions.

2. Clarifying questions: Ask clarifying questions to ensure that you have a clear understanding of your customer's needs.

3. Probing questions: Ask probing questions to uncover underlying needs or concerns that your customer may not have mentioned.

4. Leading questions: Use leading questions to guide your customer towards a solution that meets their needs.

The Standup Salesman Approach

The standup salesman approach combines active listening and questioning to create a personalized sales pitch that meets the customer's needs. Here are the steps of the standup salesman approach:

1. Build rapport: Establish a connection with your customer by showing interest in their needs and concerns.

2. Gather information: Use active listening and questioning to gather information about your customer's needs and concerns.

3. Tailor your pitch: Use the information you have gathered to tailor your pitch to meet your customer's needs.

4. Overcome objections: Use active listening and questioning to address any objections your customer may have.

5. Close the deal: Use active listening and questioning to determine when the time is right to ask for the sale.

The active listening and questioning approach of a standup salesman is essential for success in sales. By actively listening to your customers and asking the right questions, you can tailor your pitch to meet their needs and build long-term relationships. Whether you're a seasoned sale professional or just starting out, these tips can help you to become a standup salesman and close more deals.

Overcoming Objections in Global Marketing; the Approach of a Good Salesman

In the world of global marketing, overcoming objections is an essential part of the sales process. Whether you're selling a product or a service, customers will inevitably have objections that need to be addressed. In this book, we will explore the approach of a good salesman in overcoming objections in global marketing.

Understanding Objections

Facing objections is a typical situation during the process of selling. Customers may have concerns about the product or service being offered, the price, or the company itself. Understanding these objections is the first step in overcoming them.

Here are some common objections in global marketing:

1. Price: Customers may feel that the price is too high for the value they are receiving.

2. Quality: Customers may have concerns about the quality of the product or service being offered.

3. Competition: Customers may be considering other options in the market.

4. Trust: Customers may have concerns about the reputation of the company or the salesperson.

The Good Salesman Approach

A good salesman knows how to overcome objections and turn them into opportunities. Here are some tips for overcoming objections in global marketing:

1. Listen: Listen carefully to your customer's objections. Show empathy and understanding.

2. Acknowledge: Acknowledge the customer's concerns and show that you take them seriously.

3. Clarify: Clarify the objection to ensure that you understand it fully.

4. Address: Address the objection directly. Provide information or evidence that addresses the customer's concerns.

5. Reframe: Reframe the objection as an opportunity. Demonstrate how an objection can be transformed into a positive aspect.

6. Close: Close the deal by asking for the sale. Use trial closes to gauge the customer's interest and ask for the sale when the time is right.

Global Marketing Considerations

In global marketing, there are additional considerations when it comes to overcoming objections. Here are some tips for addressing objections in a global context:

1. Cultural differences: Be aware of cultural differences and adjust your approach accordingly.

2. Language barriers: Use clear and simple language to avoid misunderstandings.

3. Time zones: Be aware of time zone differences and adjust your communication accordingly.

4. Local regulations: Be aware of local regulations and ensure that your product or service complies with local laws.

In conclusion, overcoming objections is an essential part of the sales process in global marketing. By listening to your customers, acknowledging their concerns, addressing objections directly, reframing objections as opportunities, and closing the deal, you can turn objections into opportunities and build long-term relationships with your customers. Whether you're a seasoned sale professional or just starting out, these tips can help you to become a good salesman and overcome objections in global marketing

Closing the Sale: Techniques for Success

Closing the sale is the main objective of sales pitch. Whether you're selling a product or a service, the ability to close the deal is essential for success in sales. In this book, we will explore techniques for closing the sale and increasing your success as a salesperson.

Understanding the Sales Process

Before we dive into techniques for closing the sale, it's important to understand the sales process. The usual steps involved in the sales process are as follows:

1. Prospecting involves the process of pinpointing individuals or organizations who have the potential to become interested in your product or service.

2. Qualifying: Determining whether a prospect is a good fit for your product or service.

3. Presenting: Presenting your product or service to the prospect.

4. Addressing objections: Addressing any objections or concerns the prospect may have.

STANDUP SALESPERSON:
Crafting a Winning Strategy for Lasting Business Relationships

5. Closing: Asking for the sale and finalizing the deal.

Closing Techniques

Here are some techniques for closing the sale:

1. The assumptive close: This technique involves assuming that the customer is ready to buy and asking for the sale.

2. The urgency close: This technique involves creating a sense of urgency to encourage the customer to buy now.

3. The alternative close: This technique involves presenting the customer with two options, both of which lead to a sale.

4. The trial close: This technique involves asking for the sale in a non-threatening way to gauge the customer's interest.

5. The objection close: This technique involves addressing any objections the customer may have and then asking for the sale.

Tips for Successful Closing

STANDUP
SALESPERSON:
Crafting a Winning Strategy for Lasting Business Relationships

Here are some tips for successful closing

1. Build rapport: Establish a connection with your customer by showing interest in their needs and concerns

2. Create urgency: Use urgency to encourage the customer to make a decision now.

3. Be confident: Believe in your product or service and convey that confidence to the customer.

4. Address objections: Address any objections the customer may have to remove barriers to the sale.

5. Ask for the sale: Be direct and ask for the sale when the time is right.

Concluding the sale is a crucial aspect of the sales procedure. By using techniques such as the assumptive close, the urgency close, the alternative close, the trial close, and the objection close, you can increase your success as a salesperson and close more deals. By building rapport, creating urgency, being confident, addressing objections, and asking for the sale, you can become a successful closer and achieve your sales goals.

LEVERAGING TECHNOLOGY

In the present era of digitalization, technology has become an indispensable component of our everyday routine. From smart phones to cloud computing, technology has revolutionized the way we work, communicate, and interact with the world around us. For businesses and organizations, leveraging technology has become a crucial part of staying competitive in the industry.

Leveraging technology refers to the strategic use of technology to improve business operations, processes, and customer experience. By integrating technology into their operations, businesses and organizations can automate tasks, increase productivity, and reduce costs. For example, businesses can use customer relationship management (CRM) software to manage customer interactions and improve customer experience. They can also use enterprise resource planning (ERP) software to manage their supply chain and inventory.

STANDUP
SALESPERSON:
Crafting a Winning Strategy for Lasting Business Relationships

The benefits of leveraging technology are numerous. Enhanced efficiency is considered one of the most noteworthy advantages. By automating tasks, businesses and organizations can reduce the need for manual labor and increase productivity. Additionally, technology can improve communication and collaboration, allowing teams to work together more effectively. Improving decision-making and problem-solving skills can result in faster and better outcomes.

Another benefit of leveraging technology is improved customer experience. Technology can be used to personalize interactions with customers, providing them with a more personalized experience. For example, businesses can use data analytics to analyze customer behavior and preferences, and then use this information to provide tailored recommendations and promotions.

Finally, leveraging technology can help businesses and organizations stay competitive in their respective industries. By staying up-to-date on the latest technological advancements and trends, businesses can gain a competitive edge and stay ahead of the competition.

Nevertheless, utilizing technology also poses certain difficulties. One of the issues is cyber security. As businesses and organizations become more reliant on technology, they become more vulnerable to cyber attacks. It is important to set up solid security controls to protect against these threats. Another challenge is the cost of implementing and maintaining technology. Businesses and organizations must carefully consider their budget and resources before investing in technology. Finally, staff training and adoption can also be a challenge. It is important to provide adequate training and support to ensure that staff members can effectively use the technology.

To overcome these challenges, businesses and organizations must follow best practices. These include regularly evaluating and updating technology, implementing strong security measures, and providing adequate staff training and support. It is also important to consider the impact of technology on customers and to ensure that technology is being used to improve customer experience. Leveraging technology is essential for businesses and organizations to stay competitive in today's fast-paced world. By integrating technology into their operations and following best practices, businesses can improve efficiency, customer experience, and stay ahead of the competition.

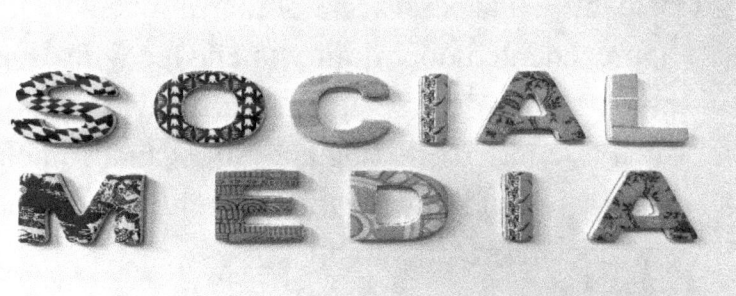

Utilizing Social Media and Digital Marketing

In today's digital age, social media and digital marketing have become essential tools for businesses and organizations to reach their target audience and promote their products and services. Social media platforms such as Facebook, Twitter, and Instagram, as well as digital marketing techniques such as email marketing and search engine optimization (SEO), have revolutionized the way businesses and organizations market and advertise themselves.

One of the biggest advantages of utilizing social media and digital marketing is the ability to reach

STANDUP
SALESPERSON:
Crafting a Winning Strategy for Lasting Business Relationships

a large and diverse audience. Social media platforms have billions of users worldwide, providing businesses and organizations with an unprecedented opportunity to engage with potential customers. Digital marketing techniques such as email marketing and SEO can also help businesses and organizations reach their target audience more effectively.

Another advantage of utilizing social media and digital marketing is the ability to personalize marketing and advertising efforts. Social media platforms allow businesses and organizations to create targeted ads and promotions based on user data such as age, gender, location, and interests. This can lead to more effective marketing and advertising campaigns, as businesses and organizations can tailor their messages to specific audiences.

Utilizing social media and digital marketing also allows businesses and organizations to track and analyze their marketing efforts. Social media platforms and digital marketing tools provide businesses and organizations with detailed analytics and insights into their campaigns,

STANDUP
SALESPERSON:
Crafting a Winning Strategy for Lasting Business Relationships

allowing them to measure the effectiveness of their efforts and make data-driven decisions.

However, utilizing social media and digital marketing also comes with its own set of challenges. One of the biggest challenges is the need to stay up-to-date on the latest trends and best practices. Social media platforms and digital marketing techniques are constantly evolving, and businesses and organizations must stay informed and adapt to changes in order to remain competitive.

Another challenge is the need to create high-quality and engaging content. Social media users are inundated with content on a daily basis, and businesses and organizations must create content that stands out and captures their audience's attention. This requires creativity, strong writing skills, and a deep understanding of the target audience.

To effectively utilize social media and digital marketing, businesses and organizations must follow best practices. These include creating a strong brand presence on social media, creating high-quality and engaging content, targeting the right audience, and tracking and analyzing their marketing efforts. It is also important to stay up-to-date on the latest trends and best practices, and to adapt to changes in the industry.

Obviously, utilizing social media and digital marketing is essential for businesses and organizations to reach their target audience and promote their products and services. By creating a strong brand presence on social media, creating high-quality and engaging content, targeting the right audience, and tracking and analyzing their marketing efforts, businesses and organizations can effectively utilize social media and digital marketing to stay competitive in the industry.

Implementing CRM Software

In today's business world, customer relationship management (CRM) software is an essential tool for businesses of all sizes. CRM software helps businesses manage their interactions with customers, track customer data, and automate sales processes. Implementing CRM software can be a complex process, but it is critical to the success of any business that wants to improve customer relationships and increase sales.

In this chapter, we will discuss the steps involved in implementing CRM software in your business. We will cover everything from choosing the right software to training your employees and ensuring that the software is being used effectively.

Step 1: Define Your Goals

Before you can begin implementing CRM software, it is essential to define your goals. What are your objectives for the software? Are you looking to improve customer satisfaction, increase sales, or streamline your sales processes? Defining your goals will help you choose the right software and ensure that you are using it effectively.

Step 2: Choose the Right Software

Once you have defined your goals, it is time to choose the right CRM software for your business. There are many options available, and it is essential to choose software that meets your specific needs. Consider factors such as the size of your business, the complexity of your sales processes, and your budget.

Step 3: Plan the Implementation

Once you have chosen the right software, it is time to plan the implementation. This involves developing a timeline, identifying key stakeholders, and assigning responsibilities. It is also essential to establish a budget and ensure that you have the resources necessary to implement the software successfully.

Step 4: Train Your Employees

Implementing CRM software requires the support of your employees. It is essential to provide adequate training to ensure that your employees understand how to use the software effectively. This could entail conducting training sessions, creating user manuals, and providing continuous support.

Step 5: Ensure User Adoption

One of the biggest challenges in implementing CRM software is ensuring user adoption. It is essential to communicate the benefits of the software to your employees and encourage them to use it. This may involve offering incentives, developing a rewards program, or providing ongoing training and support.

Step 6: Monitor and Evaluate

Once the software is implemented, it is essential to monitor and evaluate its effectiveness. This involves tracking key metrics such as customer satisfaction, sales, and user adoption. Use this information to identify areas for improvement and make adjustments as necessary.

Implementing CRM software is a critical step for businesses that want to improve customer relationships and increase sales. By defining your goals, choosing the right software, planning the implementation, training your employees, ensuring user adoption, and monitoring and evaluating the effectiveness of the software, you can successfully implement CRM software in your business.

Automating Sales Processes

The use of sales automation has become crucial for businesses seeking to enhance their efficiency and productivity in the current fast-paced business environment. Automating sales processes involves using technology to streamline the sales process, from lead generation to closing the sale. This article aims to provide a comprehensive guide on how businesses can effectively automate their sales processes to increase their revenue and profitability.

Understanding Sales Automation

Sales automation involves using technology to automate repetitive and time-consuming tasks involved in the sales process. This includes tasks such as lead generation, lead nurturing, follow-up, and closing the sale. Sales teams can concentrate on more strategic activities like fostering customer relationships and finalizing deals by automating these tasks.

Benefits of Sales Automation

The benefits of sales automation are numerous. Firstly, it reduces the time and effort required to complete repetitive tasks, allowing sales teams to focus on more strategic tasks. Secondly, it increases the efficiency and productivity of the sales process, resulting in increased revenue and profitability. Thirdly, it improves the accuracy and consistency of the sales process, reducing errors and increasing customer satisfaction.

Implementing Sales Automation

To implement sales automation, businesses need to identify the key areas of the sales process that can be automated. This includes lead generation, lead nurturing, follow-up, and closing the sale. Once identified, businesses need to select the appropriate technology to automate these tasks. This includes customer relationship management (CRM) software, marketing automation software, and sales automation software.

Best Practices for Sales Automation

To ensure the success of sales automation, businesses need to follow best practices. This includes defining clear goals and objectives for the sales process, selecting the appropriate technology, training sales teams on how to use the technology, and regularly reviewing and optimizing the sales process.

Challenges of Sales Automation

While sales automation offers many benefits, there are also challenges that businesses need to be aware of. These include the cost of implementing and maintaining the technology, the need for ongoing training and support, and the potential for resistance from sales teams who may be resistant to change.

Measuring the Success of Sales Automation

To measure the success of sales automation, businesses need to define clear metrics and KPIs. This includes metrics such as lead generation, conversion rates, and sales revenue. By regularly tracking these metrics, businesses can identify areas for improvement and optimize their sales process for maximum efficiency and profitability.

Sales automation is an essential tool for businesses looking to increase their efficiency and productivity. By automating repetitive and time-consuming tasks, sales teams can focus on more strategic tasks and increase their revenue and profitability. However, to ensure the success of sales automation, businesses need to follow best practices, regularly review and optimize their sales process, and measure their success using clear metrics and KPIs.

Here are some steps to automating sales processes:

Step 1: Understand Sales Automation

To begin, it's important to understand what sales automation is and how it can benefit your business. This step involves learning about the tasks that can be automated, such as lead generation, lead nurturing, follow-up, and closing the sale.

Step 2: Identify Key Areas for Automation

Next, you need to identify the key areas of your sales process that can be automated. This involves analyzing your current sales process and identifying the repetitive and time-consuming tasks that can be automated.

Step 3: Select the Right Technology

Once you've identified the areas of your sales process that can be automated, you need to select the appropriate technology to automate these tasks. This includes customer relationship management (CRM) software, marketing automation software, and sales automation software.

Step 4: Implement Sales Automation

With the technology in place, it's time to implement sales automation. This involves training your sales team on how to use the technology and integrating it into your existing sales process.

Step 5: Follow Best Practices

To ensure the success of sales automation, it's important to follow best practices. This includes defining clear goals and objectives for the sales process, regularly reviewing and optimizing the sales process, and providing ongoing training and support to your sales team.

Step 6: Measure Success

Finally, you need to measure the success of your sales automation efforts. This involves defining clear metrics and KPIs, tracking these metrics over time, and using this data to identify areas for improvement and optimize your sales process for maximum efficiency and profitability.

BUILDING AND MAINTAINING RELATIONSHIPS

Building and maintaining business relationships is crucial for the success of any organization. Strong relationships with customers, suppliers, and partners can lead to increased sales, improved reputation, and new opportunities. In this article, we will discuss the importance of building and maintaining business relationships and the ways to do it effectively.

Importance of Building and Maintaining Business Relationships

Business relationships can provide numerous benefits to organizations. Here are some reasons why building and maintaining business relationships are essential:

1. Increased Sales

Strong business relationships can lead to increased sales. When customers trust and respect a business, they are more likely to purchase their products or services. Building a strong relationship with customers can also lead to repeat business and referrals.

2. Improved Reputation

Business relationships can also contribute to a company's reputation. Positive relationships with customers, suppliers, and partners can enhance a company's image and increase its credibility. A good reputation can attract new customers and opportunities.

3. New Opportunities

Building and maintaining business relationships can also lead to new opportunities. Collaborating with partners and suppliers can provide access to new markets, technologies, and resources. Strong relationships with customers can also lead to new product ideas and feedback.

4. Competitive Advantage

Strong business relationships can provide a competitive advantage. When a business has a strong network of relationships, it can respond quickly to changes in the market and adapt to new challenges. Relationships can also provide access to unique resources and expertise.

Ways to Build and Maintain Business Relationships

Building and maintaining business relationships require effort and commitment. Find below ways to do this effectively:

1. Communication

Effective communication is crucial for building and maintaining business relationships. It is essential to listen actively, express yourself clearly, and be open to feedback. Good communication can help resolve conflicts, build trust, and strengthen bonds.

2. Deliver on Promises

Delivering on promises is a crucial aspect of building and maintaining business relationships. It is essential to be reliable and follow through on commitments. Consistently delivering on promises can build trust and strengthen relationships.

3. Personalize Interactions

Personalizing interactions with customers, suppliers, and partners can help build strong relationships. It is essential to understand their needs and preferences and tailor interactions accordingly. Personalized interactions can create a positive and memorable experience and build loyalty.

4. Offer Value

Offering value is an essential aspect of building and maintaining business relationships. Providing high-quality products or services, offering competitive pricing, and providing excellent customer service can build trust and strengthen relationships.

5. Consistency

Consistency is key to building and maintaining business relationships. It is essential to stay in touch regularly and make time for each other. Consistency can help build trust and strengthen bonds over time.

Building and maintaining business relationships are crucial for the success of any organization. It requires effort, commitment, and effective communication. By prioritizing relationships with customers, suppliers, and partners, businesses can gain a competitive advantage, increase sales and access new opportunities.

Following Up With Customers

Following up with customers is an essential part of any business. It is a way of showing your customers that you care about their satisfaction and that you want to build a long-term relationship with them. Following up also helps to identify any issues or concerns that the customer may have, allowing you to address them before they become bigger problems. In this article, we will discuss the importance of following up with customers and provide some tips on how to do it effectively.

Why is following up with customers important?

1. It shows that you care

Following up with customers clearly shows that you care about their satisfaction and that you are willing to go the extra mile to ensure that they are happy with your product or service. Establishing trust and loyalty through this approach can result in repeated business and recommendations.

2. It helps to identify issues

Following up with customers can help to identify any issues or concerns that they may have. This gives you the opportunity to address these issues before they become bigger problems, which can help to prevent negative reviews and damage to your reputation.

3. It provides valuable feedback

Following up with customers can provide valuable feedback that you can use to improve your product or service. This feedback can help you to identify areas where you are doing well and areas where you need to improve.

Tips for following up with customers

1. Be timely

When following up with customers, it is important to be timely. This means following up shortly after the customer has made a purchase or had an interaction with your business. This shows that you are on top of things and that you value their time.

2. Be personal

When following up with customers, it is important to be personal. This means addressing them by name and using a tone that is friendly and conversational. This can help to build a rapport with the customer and make them feel valued.

3. Ask for feedback

When following up with customers, it is important to ask for feedback. This can be done through a survey or a simple email asking for their thoughts on their experience with your business. This feedback can help you to identify areas where you need to improve and areas where you are doing well.

4. Offer a solution

When following up with customers, it is important to offer a solution to any issues or concerns that they may have. This can be done by providing a refund, offering a discount on their next purchase, or simply apologizing for any inconvenience that they may have experienced.

5. Follow up again

When following up with customers, it is important to follow up again. This can be done a few days or weeks after the initial follow-up to ensure that the customer is still satisfied with your product or service. This shows that you are committed to their satisfaction and that you value their business.

In conclusion, following up with customers is an essential part of any business. It shows that you care about their satisfaction, helps to identify issues, and provides valuable feedback. By following the tips outlined in this article, you can effectively follow up with your customers and build long-term relationships that lead to repeat business and referrals.

Providing Exceptional Customer Service

Providing exceptional customer service is a crucial aspect of any successful business. This is the foundation upon which customer loyalty and retention are excelling. Exceptional customer service involves going above and beyond to meet the needs of your customers and exceed their expectations. In this article, we will discuss the importance of providing exceptional customer service and provide some tips on how to do it effectively.

Why is providing exceptional customer service important?

1. Builds customer loyalty

Providing exceptional customer service builds customer loyalty. Valuing and appreciating your customers can result in higher customer retention and referrals, thereby boosting your business's sales and revenue.

2. Increases customer retention

STANDUP
SALESPERSON:
Crafting a Winning Strategy for Lasting Business Relationships

Providing exceptional customer service increases customer retention. When customers have an amazing experience with your services, It is likely they are going to remain in your business lane. This can lead to long-term relationships that are beneficial for both the customer and the business.

3. Improves brand reputation

Providing customers with polite experience can trigger them to spread the word about your business, leading to favorable word-of-mouth advertising and heightened brand recognition.

Tips for providing exceptional customer service

1. Be responsive

Being responsive is a key aspect of providing exceptional customer service. Being prompt in addressing customer inquiries and issues demonstrates your respect for their time and dedication to fulfilling their requirements.

2. Be knowledgeable

Being knowledgeable about your product or service is important when providing exceptional customer service. This means being able to answer customer questions and provide helpful information. It shows that you are an expert in your field and can be trusted to provide accurate information.

3. Be friendly

Being friendly is an important aspect of providing exceptional customer service. This means greeting customers with a smile and a positive attitude. It shows that you value their business and are committed to providing a positive experience.

4. Go above and beyond

Going above and beyond is a key aspect of providing exceptional customer service. This means doing more than what is expected to meet the needs of your customers. It shows that you are committed to their satisfaction and are willing to go the extra mile to exceed their expectations.

5. Follow up

Following up is an important aspect of providing exceptional customer service. This means following up with customers after a purchase to ensure that they are satisfied with their experience.

It shows that you value their feedback and are committed to their satisfaction.

Providing exceptional customer service is a crucial aspect of any successful business. It builds customer loyalty, increases customer retention, and improves brand reputation. By being responsive, knowledgeable, friendly, going above and beyond, and following up, you can provide exceptional customer service that will keep good track of your customers.

Creating a Referral Program

Creating a referral program as a standup salesman can be an effective way to generate new business and increase sales. Referral programs are a great way to leverage your existing customer base to reach new customers and increase your sales pipeline. In this article, we will discuss how to create a referral program as a standup salesman.

1. Define your program goals

Before you start creating your referral program, it's important to define your program goals. What are your objectives for the referral program? Are you aiming to enhance sales, generate leads, or accomplish both? By defining your goals, you can design a program that is customized to meet your specific requirements.

2. Determine your incentives

Offering incentives is a vital component of a successful word-of-mouth marketing program. You need to determine what incentives you will offer to your customers for referring new business to you. The incentives to offer may include discounts on their next purchase, complementary products or services, or even monetary rewards. Whatever incentives you choose, make sure they are attractive enough to motivate your customers to refer new business to you.

3. Create a referral process

Once you have defined your program goals and incentives, it's time to create a referral process.

STANDUP
SALESPERSON:
Crafting a Winning Strategy for Lasting Business Relationships

This is the step-by-step process that your customers will follow to refer new business to you. Make sure your referral process is simple and easy to understand. Provide clear instructions on how to refer new business to you, and make it easy for your customers to do so.

4. Promote your referral program

Promoting your referral program is key to its success. You need to make sure your customers are aware of your program and understand the incentives and referral process. Use your website, social media, and email marketing to promote your referral program. You can also create flyers or other marketing materials to distribute to your customers.

5. Monitor and track your results

Once your referral program is up and running, it's important to monitor and track your results. This will help you determine the effectiveness of your program and make any necessary adjustments. Use analytics tools to track the number of referrals you receive, the conversion rate of those referrals, and the overall impact on your sales pipeline.

Creating a referral program as a standup salesman can be an effective way to generate new business and increase sales. By defining your program goals, determining your incentives, creating a referral process, promoting your program, and monitoring your results, you can create a successful referral program that will help you grow your business.

ANALYZING AND ADJUSTING YOUR STRATEGY AS A STANDUP SALESMAN

As a salesperson, it is essential to have a well-thought-out strategy to achieve your sales goals. However, even the best strategy may not work in all situations. Therefore, it is crucial to analyze and adjust your strategy when necessary to ensure that you are on track to meet your targets.

Analyzing Your Strategy

To analyze your strategy, you need to evaluate your sales performance regularly. This evaluation should be based on your sales data, including the number of leads, conversions, and revenue generated. By analyzing your sales data, you can identify the areas where your strategy is working and those that need improvement.

One way to analyze your strategy is to identify the sales channels that are generating the most revenue. This could be through phone calls, emails, or face-to-face meetings. Once you have identified the most effective sales channels, you can focus your efforts on them and adjust your strategy to maximize their potential.

Another way to analyze your strategy is to identify the types of customers that are most likely to buy your product or service. This could be based on their demographics, behavior, or interests. By understanding your target audience, you can tailor your sales approach to meet their needs and preferences.

Adjusting Your Strategy

Once you have analyzed your sales data and identified the areas that need improvement, it is time to adjust your strategy. This could involve making changes to your sales approach, sales channels, or target audience.

For example, if you find that your sales approach is not resonating with your target audience, you may need to adjust your messaging or tone. If you find that a particular sales channel is not generating enough revenue, you may need to explore other channels or adjust your approach to make it more effective.

It is essential to be flexible and open to change when adjusting your strategy. Sometimes, the changes you make may not have an immediate impact on your sales performance. However, over time, these changes can help you achieve your sales goals.

Analyzing and adjusting your sales strategy is essential to achieving your sales goals. By regularly evaluating your sales data and making adjustments when necessary, you can ensure that you are on track to meet your targets. Remember to be flexible and open to change when adjusting your strategy, as this can help you achieve long-term success as a standup salesman.

Tracking Sales Metrics

As a standup salesman, it is crucial to track your sales metrics to measure your performance and identify areas for improvement. Sales metrics are key performance indicators (KPIs) that help you understand how well you are doing in achieving your sales goals. By tracking sales metrics, you can make data-driven decisions that can help you optimize your sales strategy and increase revenue.

There are several sales metrics that you should track as a standup salesman. These include:

1. Lead Generation Metrics: These metrics help you track the number of leads you generate and the quality of those leads. Examples of lead generation metrics include website traffic, social media engagement, and email open rates.

2. Conversion Metrics: These metrics help you track the number of leads that convert into customers. Examples of conversion metrics include conversion rates, sales cycle length, and win rates.

3. Revenue Metrics: These metrics help you track the amount of revenue you generate from your sales efforts. Examples of revenue metrics include total sales revenue, average deal size, and customer lifetime value.

4. Customer Satisfaction Metrics: These metrics help you track how satisfied your customers are with your product or service. Examples of customer satisfaction metrics include Net Promoter Score (NPS), customer retention rate, and customer feedback.

Analyzing Customer Feedback

In addition to tracking sales metrics, it is essential to analyze customer feedback to understand how you can improve your sales strategy. Customer feedback can provide valuable insights into what your customers like and dislike about your product or service, and how you can better meet their needs.

One way to analyze customer feedback is to conduct surveys or interviews with your customers. This can help you understand their pain points, preferences, and expectations. You can also use social media monitoring tools to track what customers are saying about your brand online.

Improving Your Sales Strategy

Once you have tracked your sales metrics and analyzed customer feedback, it is time to continuously improve your sales strategy. This could involve making changes to your sales approach, sales channels, or target audience. For example, if you find that your conversion rates are low, you may need to adjust your sales messaging or offer a promotion to incentivize customers to buy.

Tracking sales metrics, analyzing customer feedback, and continuously improving your sales strategy are essential to achieving success as a standup salesman. By using data-driven insights to optimize your sales approach, you can increase revenue, improve customer satisfaction, and build a strong reputation in your industry.

Analyzing Customer Feedback

As a standup salesman, it is essential to analyze customer feedback to improve your sales strategy and increase revenue. Customer feedback provides valuable insights into what your customers like and dislike about your product or service, and how you can better meet their needs.

There are several ways to analyze customer feedback as a standup salesman. These include:

1. Conducting Surveys: Surveys are a useful tool for collecting customer feedback. They can be conducted online or in-person and can be customized to ask specific questions about your product or service. Analyzing the quantitative data obtained from surveys can help in identifying trends and patterns.

2. Monitoring Social Media: Social media platforms like Twitter, Facebook, and Instagram provide a wealth of customer feedback. By monitoring these platforms, you can track what customers are saying about your brand, identify common complaints or issues, and respond to customers in real-time.

3. Analyzing Reviews: Reviews on sites like Yelp, Google, and Amazon can provide valuable insights into what customers like and dislike about your product or service. By analyzing reviews, you can identify common themes and areas for improvement.

4. Conducting Interviews: Interviews with customers can provide in-depth insights into their experiences with your product or service. Interviews can be conducted in-person or over the phone and can be used to gather qualitative data about customer preferences and pain points.

Once you have collected customer feedback, it is essential to analyze it to identify areas for improvement. This could involve making changes to your product or service, adjusting your sales approach, or improving your customer service.

For example, if you find that customers are consistently complaining about a specific feature of your product, you may need to make changes to that feature to better meet their needs. If you find that customers are having difficulty navigating your website, you may need to make changes to improve the user experience.

As a Standup Salesman, analyzing customer feedback is essential to achieving success as a standup salesman. By using customer feedback to improve your product or service, you can increase customer satisfaction, build brand loyalty, and ultimately increase revenue.

Continuously Improving Your Sales Strategy

As a standup salesman, it is essential to continuously improve your sales strategy to increase revenue and achieve your sales goals. Improving your sales strategy involves making data-driven decisions, optimizing your sales approach, and staying up-to-date with industry trends.

There are several ways to continuously improve your sales strategy as a standup salesman. These include:

1. Tracking Sales Metrics: Tracking sales metrics is essential to understanding how well you are doing in achieving your sales goals. By tracking metrics like lead generation, conversion rates, and revenue, you can identify areas for improvement and make data-driven decisions to optimize your sales approach.

2. Analyzing Customer Feedback: Analyzing customer feedback is crucial to understanding what your customers like and dislike about your product or service. By analyzing customer feedback, you

STANDUP SALESPERSON:
Crafting a Winning Strategy for Lasting Business Relationships

can identify common pain points and make changes to better meet their needs.

3. Staying Up-to-Date with Industry Trends: Staying up-to-date with industry trends is essential to remaining competitive in your industry. Staying up-to-date with the latest trends and technologies can help you discover new growth opportunities and maintain a competitive edge.

4. Continuous Learning: Continuous learning is essential to improving your sales strategy. By attending sales training and workshops, reading industry publications, and networking with other sales professionals, you can gain new insights and skills that can help you improve your sales approach.

Once you have identified areas for improvement, it is essential to make changes to your sales strategy. This could involve making changes to your sales approach, sales channels, or target audience. For example, if you find that your conversion rates are low, you may need to adjust your sales messaging or offer a promotion to incentivize customers to buy.

Continuously improving your sales strategy is essential to achieving success as a standup salesman. By making data-driven decisions, analyzing customer feedback, staying up-to-date with industry trends, and continuously learning, you can optimize your sales approach, increase revenue, and build a strong reputation in your industry.

50 General Acts of a Good Salesperson

Here are some acts of a standup salesman.

1. Always be punctual and arrive early to meetings..

2. Dress professionally and appropriately for each meeting.

3. Research your client's business and industry before each meeting.

4. Listen attentively to your client's needs and concerns.

5. Ask open-ended questions to better understand your client's needs.

6. Present solutions that specifically address your client's needs.

7. Use storytelling to make your presentations more engaging.

8. Use humor strategically to build rapport with clients.

9. Keep your presentations concise and to the point.

10. Use visuals and props to enhance your presentations.

11. Use testimonials and case studies to build credibility.

12. Follow up promptly after each meeting to show your dedication.

13. *Keep detailed records of your interactions with clients.*

14. *Use social media to build your personal brand and connect with clients.*

15. *Attend industry events to network and stay up-to-date.*

16. *Continuously educate yourself on your industry and products.*

17. *Set clear goals and track your progress.*

18. *Be persistent, but also know when to back off.*

19. *Use objections as an opportunity to address concerns and build trust.*

20. *Build relationships with gatekeepers and assistants.*

STANDUP
SALESPERSON:
Crafting a Winning Strategy for Lasting Business Relationships

21. Use email and phone communication effectively.

22. Use video conferencing to save time and money.

23. Be flexible and adaptable to different personalities and communication styles.

24. Use language that resonates with your client's values and goals.

25. Show empathy and understanding towards your client's challenges.

26. Use social proof to demonstrate your value and expertise.

27. Create a sense of urgency by utilizing scarcity and urgency tactics.

29. Use the power of storytelling to create emotional connections.

30. Use humor to lighten the mood and build rapport.

31. Use active listening to show your client that you care.

32. Use mirroring and matching to build rapport and trust.

33. Use social media to connect with prospects and build relationships.

34. Use referral marketing to expand your network and build trust.

35. Use content marketing to educate and inform your prospects.

36. Use webinars and online events to reach a wider audience.

37. Use game-based learning to engage and motivate your prospects.

38. Use personalized messaging to show your prospects that you care. 39. Use social proof to demonstrate your expertise and credibility.

40. Use data and analytics to track your progress and optimize your approach.

41. Use video marketing to showcase your products and services.

42. Use email marketing to nurture your leads and build relationships.

43. Use discretion when automating your lead generation and customer service.

44. Use artificial intelligence to personalize your approach and improve your results.

45. Use customer feedback to improve your products and services.

46. Use customer service as a way to build loyalty and trust.

47. Use up selling and cross-selling to increase your revenue.

48. Use strategic partnerships to expand your reach and build credibility.

49. Use customer referrals to grow your business organically.

50. Use continuous learning and improvement to stay ahead of the competition.

CONCLUSION

"The Standup Salesperson: Crafting a Winning Strategy for Lasting Business Relationships" provides a comprehensive guide to mastering the art of sales. By building a strong foundation, crafting a compelling message, mastering sales techniques, leveraging technology, building and maintaining relationships, and analyzing and adjusting your strategy, you can become a successful standup salesman who not only meets but exceeds their sales goals.

Throughout this book, we have emphasized the importance of having a sales strategy and making data-driven decisions to optimize your approach. By tracking sales metrics, analyzing customer feedback, and continuously improving your sales strategy, you can increase revenue, improve customer satisfaction, and build a strong reputation in your industry.

We encourage you to implement the sales strategies and techniques outlined in this book and to continuously learn and adapt to the changing landscape of sales. Remember to prioritize building lasting relationships with your customers, as they are the key to long-term success as a standup salesman.

By following the guidance in this book, you can become a standup salesman who not only achieves their sales goals but also builds lasting relationships with their customers.

Recap of Key Takeaways

"The Standup Salesperson: Crafting a Winning Strategy for Lasting Business Relationships" is a comprehensive guide that helps in mastering the art of sales. The book provides some key takeaways, which are:

1. Building a Strong Foundation: Understanding your product or service, identifying your target audience, and researching the competition are essential to building a strong foundation for your sales strategy.

2. Crafting Your Message: Creating a unique value proposition, developing a compelling pitch, and using storytelling to connect with customers can help you stand out from the competition.

3. Mastering Sales Techniques: Active listening and questioning, overcoming objections, and closing the sale are essential sales techniques that can help you close more deals.

4. Leveraging Technology: Utilizing social media and digital marketing, implementing CRM software, and automating sales processes can help you streamline your sales approach and reach more customers.

5. Building and Maintaining Relationships: Following up with customers, providing exceptional customer service, and creating a referral program can help you build lasting relationships with your customers.

6. Analyzing and Adjusting Your Strategy: Tracking sales metrics, analyzing customer feedback, and continuously improving your sales strategy are essential to achieving success as a standup salesman.

By implementing the strategies and techniques outlined in this book, you can become a successful standup salesman who not only meets but exceeds their sales goals. Remember to make data-driven decisions, continuously learn and adapt to the changing landscape of sales, and always prioritize building lasting relationships with your customers.

Encouragement to Implement Sales Strategies and Techniques

"The Standup Salesperson: Crafting a Winning Strategy for Lasting Business Relationships" provides a comprehensive guide to mastering the art of sales. Throughout the book, we have emphasized the importance of having a sales strategy and making data-driven decisions to optimize your approach.

We encourage you to implement the sales strategies and techniques outlined in this book. You can increase your revenue, improve customer satisfaction, and build a strong reputation in your industry. Remember to prioritize building lasting relationships with your customers, as they are the key to long-term success as a standup salesman.

It is essential to continuously learn and adapt to the changing landscape of sales. Attend sales training and workshops, read industry publications, and network with other sales professionals to gain new insights and skills that can help you improve your sales approach.

By implementing the strategies and techniques outlined in this book, you can become a standup salesman who not only achieves their sales goals but also builds lasting relationships with their customers. Don't be afraid to try new approaches, experiment with different sales channels, and continuously improve your sales strategy.

STANDUP SALESPERSON:
Crafting a Winning Strategy for Lasting Business Relationships

In conclusion, we encourage you to take action and implement the sales strategies and techniques outlined in this book. With dedication, hard work, and a willingness to learn, you can become a successful standup salesman who builds lasting relationships with their customers and achieves their sales goals.

ACKNOWLEDGEMENT

I acknowledge and thank the following individuals for their support and contributions to my new book, Standup Salesperson: Crafting a Winning Strategy for Lasting Business Relationship:

1. Ravindra Dabiru
2. Carmen Murphy
3. Maria Cecilia Conde
4. Marlene Foster
5. Pat Ritter (Pat Ritter Books)
6. Liga Chacon Hernandez
7. Liliana Maruta
8. Muhammad Sajwani
9. Milagros Zegarra
10. Tracie Murray
11. Patricia Travis
12. Mathew Kikenny
13. Jude Sullivan
14. Mathew Warboys
15. @Booktasters
16. All the salespersons around the globe
17. JThomas Ross

Thank you for your support and for being a part of this journey with me.

APPRECIATION

I would like to express my gratitude to salespersons worldwide for their unwavering commitment and hard work. Their dedication to engaging with customers, fostering strong relationships, and generating revenue is truly commendable. I encourage them to continue advocating for their beliefs and to remember that their efforts have a tangible impact on people's lives.